Lyme Regis

MONMOUTH'S WEST COUNTRY REBELLION OF 1685

Drawings by

Ian Moore

Sue Davies

Nigel Clarke

(Front Cover courtesy
of Colway Theatre Trust)

ISBN 0 907683 17 7

Nigel J. Clarke Publications
Unit 2,
Russell House,
Lym Close,
Lyme Regis,
Dorset. DT7 3DE

Tel/Fax: 01297 442513

THE MONMOUTH REBELLION OF 1685

Today Lyme Regis nestles peacefully among the green hills of West Dorset. Back in the late 17th Century three sailing ships were anchored off-shore from the harbour, known through the centuries as the Cobb. They flew no flag, nor gave any hint as to the catastrophic events which were to follow the landing on this shore of the West Country.

Intelligence reports had reached King James II of an intended landing by his nephew and rival, James the Duke of Monmouth. Thus a watch was being kept on coastal ports with dissidents and political opponents to James II also being kept under surveillance.

The Duke of Monmouth was the illegitimate son of Charles II. He was a favourite son and with his father's help, was accepted into the Royal Court. It was rumoured that Charles had secretly married Monmouth's mother — though this was subsequently proved untrue. The Duke of Monmouth was a popular man, who many hoped would succeed Charles to the British crown. The Duke was a Protestant at a time when many feared the spread of Catholicism, but the legitimate heir to the throne was Charles's brother James, who was not as popular as Monmouth, and, he was a Catholic. It was while at court that Monmouth became involved in plots to deprive his uncle, James II, of the crown. The most notorious attempt was the Rye House Plot of 1683.

THE RYE HOUSE PLOT — 1683

Charles II, in the latter years of his reign suffered from ill health and it was thought he might die at anytime. A group of leading opponents to the enthronement of James II hatched a plot to instigate an uprising, during which James would be assassinated and the country would be freed from the spread of Popery. Monmouth was involved in the intrigue, as were many members of Parliament. The plot failed, with many of the conspirators being brought to trial and beheaded, while the more fortunate fled into exile. Monmouth was one of the lucky exiles. However, the plan proved premature, for Charles II recovered from his illness.

The Duke of Monmouth

MONMOUTH IN EXILE

Monmouth fled to the Netherlands to escape the wrath of his father. He wrote a letter apologising for his actions and seeking permission to return to the Royal Court. Charles soon relented and after only a few brief months of absence, he allowed his errant son to return.

Perhaps Monmouth would have been a reformed character, but in 1684 he was once more forced to flee when a subpoena arrived, ordering him to give evidence against his friend Hampden, concerning the latter's activities in the Rye House Plot. Monmouth's relationship with his father sank to a new low, but around 1685, just as they seemed on the point of reconcilliation Charles II died and James II was crowned the new King of England.

Monmouth wisely decided to stay away.

THE POLITICAL CLIMATE IN ENGLAND
PRIOR TO THE REBELLION

England still bore the scars of the English Civil War, and there were feelings of resentment. The restoration of the crown imposed harsh suffering on those who supported the Commonwealth cause. Non-conformist clergy were deprived of the living by the "Act of Uniformity" of 1662. Non-conformists were also barred from holding civil office and laws against dissenters were harshly enforced by the local Justices of the Peace. Meeting houses and non-conformist churches were burnt or closed down. The restored Anglican Church was seen by many as thinly disguised Popery. The elections to Parliament were manipulated to ensure a Tory majority in favour of James II. Consequently opposition was stifled.

Towns and areas of localized opposition existed across the country, especially in the South West. In 1680, Monmouth had toured parts of England including the South West. In many areas he was greeted as a hero, meeting many of the leading families, calling at great houses such as Longleat and smaller provincial estates, like Lackington House near Ilminster. At Forde Abbey near Chard, he was greeted by immense crowds and must have thought his political base was growing, as at the same time in Scotland, there was considerable unrest, a situation which augured favourably for a rebellion.

An alliance of opposition to the throne of James II made strange companions! There were former soldiers of Cromwell, now mostly in their late thirties and forties, religious groups which had been persecuted under the "Act of Uniformity" discouraging the restoration of the Anglican Church, Whig and other political opposition groups that had been deprived of their parliamentary seats and lastly, there was a republican element.

Despite heavy opposition existing to James II's rule, there was little co-ordination between the groups. However, it was hoped that Monmouth's leadership would have a unifying influence.

THE PLOTTING OF THE
MONMOUTH REBELLION

While in exile, Monmouth seemed content hunting, womanising and living with his mistress. He moved from Brussels to the Netherlands, where there was a large colony of refugees from the rule of James the Second. Many plots were discussed and hatched but the Duke of Monmouth seemed to shy away from any involvement. The pressure was considerable. The conspirators needed a leader who could be easily identified and popular with the masses. Monmouth was ideal for the task, and judging from his tours of the West Country while his father was alive, he seemed to have the support that would be so necessary if any rebellion were to succeed. Monmouth was eventually converted to the cause.

The leading conspirators were:

Nathanial Wade. A barrister from Bristol with a background of republican politics whose father had been a major in Cromwell's new model army. He was at odds with the rest of Monmouth's supporters over the proposed proclamation of Monmouth as King. Nathaniel Wade was one of Monmouth's commanders.

Robert Ferguson. A fanatical Scottish Presbyterian minister, he was also known as "The Plotter". It was Ferguson who drew up Monmouth's proclamation, and he who was most in favour of Monmouth being crowned King.

Thomas Dare. Dare was a goldsmith from Taunton and a whig politician; a man of considerable wealth and influence who had been jailed during a political campaign calling for a new parliament. He was also fined £5,000 for uttering 'seditious' words. After his release from jail he fled to the safety of Holland. He became the banker to the rebellion.

The Duke of Argyll. The duke was to lead the Scottish revolt and had already been involved in one unsuccessful attempt, as well as the Rye House Plot of 1683.

THE PREPARATION OF THE REVOLT

It was planned that there should be two landings of rebels. The first in Scotland by the Duke of Argyll, and the other in the South West led by the Duke of

Monmouth. A general uprising was to be orchestrated in the other centres across the country led by other conspirators. With the country in open revolt there would be a march on London and at last James Stuart would be deposed.

The rebels were short of money with which to purchase the necessary arms and ships needed for the crossing. Monmouth raised money from the sale and pawning of his family jewels. He even pawned the jewellery that belonged to his mistress. Other donations came from the supporting groups.

Christopher Battiscombe, a solicitor of Symondsbury (near Bridport), was dispatched on a secret mission to the West Country to co-ordinate the help of the local gentry in providing arms and horses. He was ineffectual, preferring to remain neutral during the conflict, and await the outcome.

News of the intended rebellion reached James, though how and where the uprising would take place was not known. The English army had been run down and the local militias were unreliable. The navy was reputedly large but it had in fact been starved of funds resulting in unseaworthy ships and scant crew. However, it was the navy that was to give Monmouth his biggest worry for it would be while crossing the Channel that the whole operation would be at its most vulnerable. The Duke needed to protect his supply ships if the landing were to succeed and to this end Monmouth and his supporters decided to hire the Dutch warship the "Heldevenberg" which carried 32 cannons and would at least give them some protection during the crossing. The hire charge was £5,000, the most expensive item on the Duke's list. The powder and shot carried in two other smaller vessels. The Duke of Argyll left Holland two weeks prior to Monmouth's departure, to sow the seeds of the Scottish rebellion.

King James having been forewarned tried to put diplomatic pressure on William of Orange to curtail the rebels. William feigned ignorance of the intended rebellion, and so on the 30th May 1685 Monmouth and his supporters set sail for England. By this time James had put his forces on alert. The Devon militia fearing an uprising at Exeter Fair remained in the county town, while the Dorset militia fearing a landing further to the east positioned itself at Poole. Monmouth landed between them at Lyme Regis, on the Dorset Devon border.

Monmouth's journey from Tessel in Holland to Lyme Regis was 400 miles and the trip took 10 days. On board Monmouth and his advisers worked at the plans for the rebellion. On the morning of June 10th the ships arrived in Lyme Bay, and were moored off the small coastal town of Seaton. A rowing boat from the Heldevenberg containing six men was let over the side. They landed on the beach and spoke to the fisherman who were repairing their nets and boats. The boat returned to the Heldevenberg after leaving two passengers on the beach.

THE LANDING OF MONMOUTH

The two passengers from the boat were Thomas Dare and a companion who were to make their way to Taunton. The group from the boat chatted to the local fishermen and asked them for news before re-embarking. They were told of the rebellion in Scotland led by the Duke of Argyll and probably learnt of the lack of troops in the area, who were by now deployed to the east and west.

The local customs official, Samuel Damsell then living in Chideock, a mile from Seatown, arrived on the beach later that morning. He questioned the fishermen as to the identity of the ships and the nature of the questions asked, then set off for Lyme to seek guidance from the Mayor, an ardent Royalist called Alford. Meanwhile, the harbourmaster at Lyme had rowed out to the anchored ships in a small boat. On arrival aboard the rebel frigate Heldevenberg the harbourmaster and his crew were held prisoner and questioned as to the likely reception that the rebels would meet in the town, and about the town's defences. The harbourmaster assured them that they would meet little resistance. The situation was confirmed by a passing Charmouth fisherman who came aboard the Heldevenberg to sell fish to the rebels; an act he was later hanged for.

ASHORE AT LYME

With the harbourmaster detained on the ship and the vessels anchored offshore there was little the Mayor could do. He was unsure of the exact nature of their quest. The arrival of the customs official did little to resolve the situation. Inquiries were made among other visiting sailors as to the likely nationality of the vessels, and it was speculated that they might be Dutch or French. The strong offshore wind would have made the berthing of the vessels difficult, and it was assumed that this was the reason why the vessels did not come into port. The Mayor kept a watch on the vessels, there being little else that he could do.

The ships remained offshore all day. The Mayor was suspicious though not yet alarmed. At 5 p.m. the mail coach arrived from London. Among the correspondence was a report that the Duke of Monmouth had set sail from Holland with a group of armed rebels in three vessels and their destination was presumed to be a south coast port! At last Alford realised the significance of the anchored vessels. He

11

Monmouth's landing at Lyme Regis

ordered powder to be obtained for the cannons that defended the town, and the local militia to be assembled. The nearest supply of powder was in a ship that had recently arrived from Barbados and the customs official, Damsell, was sent with helpers to fetch the powder. He reached the Cobb as the first boats came ashore from the ships. The rebels landed on the beach to the west of the Cobb, out of range of the empty town cannons. Damsell raced back to the town with the powder. Monmouth led his group along the footpath skirting the old Civil War fort which then formed part of Lyme's sea defences, and on towards the town. The town militia had fled. Only one man had answered the summons to arms and he joined the rebels! The Mayor, being a Royalist and true to James, left the scene and rode off to Honiton to inform the Crown's forces of the arrival of the Duke. Damsell, still in the town, was confused and at first thought that Monmouth had been captured by the armed group, then realised that they were Monmouth's supporters. He and his colleague left for London, instructing the local militias along the way not to allow any more rebels to join Monmouth in Lyme. The roads and bridges to the east of Lyme were patrolled. It took Damsell two days to reach London. They went to the home of Winston Churchill, whose father Lord Churchill took them for an audience with James, and they outlined the position. James rewarded them and started to orchestrate his campaign of action against the rebellious Monmouth.

MONMOUTH AT LYME REGIS

At Lyme Monmouth was hailed as the saviour of the Protestant cause. Some probably knew in advance of Monmouth's coming, though no sign of it was obvious. Most of the non-conformist leaders had already been arrested or were forced to act underground and therefore such information would have been very restricted, especially after the calamity of the failed Rye House Plot.

Monmouth raised his standard in a field to the east of the town, now entirely eroded away by the sea. The news soon spread and many men were joining him. They were divided up into regiments, each being given a different coloured sash. The Duke took possession of the forts around Lyme. The original landing party consisted of only 83 men, which, if Lyme had been better prepared could easily have been overcome. The Duke's proclamation was read in the square. This accused the King of many crimes, and declared Monmouth's true right to the crown.

(The manifesto had been printed in London by William Disney, in Flemish, French and English. Disney was arrested in London on June 15 and executed on June 29).

THE FIRST CALAMITY:
THE DEATH OF THOMAS DARE

Thomas Dare, the rebel leader who had landed at Seatown, arrived back from Taunton with a troop of locally raised cavalry. It was on this mission that Dare had obtained from Forde Abbey a particularly fine horse. Andrew Fletcher, a Scottish Laird, who Monmouth had chosen to lead the cavalry, and who was one of the few professional soldiers in his army, took possession of the animal, which upset Dare. An argument broke out whereby Dare tried to whip Fletcher, a man of known short temper. In the heat of the moment he shot Dare, and killed him. Dare was a popular local man, and Monmouth was forced to send

Fletcher off in the Heldevenberg. Thus he lost a very able man and one of the few with any military experience; moreover the death of Dare robbed him of one of his most influential supporters.

RESPONSE TO THE REBEL LANDING
BY JAMES II

In London James had ordered the arrest of all Monmouth's known contacts and his friends were questioned. A reward was offered for the taking of Monmouth, dead or alive. The sum of £400,000 was raised by Parliament for the suppression of the rebellion, and Catholic lords were instructed to raise militias. Troops were dispatched from Salisbury to reinforce the Duke of Albermarle's army at Exeter. The Devon militia was to join up with the Somerset militia, and the Dorset militia was to move on towards Lyme Regis. The king hoped to confine the rebellion to Lyme Regis, and so stem an uprising.

In Lyme, many flocked to join the Monmouth army which had little equipment, few horses for cavalry and only four field guns. Experience was lacking, though there were a few old 'ironsides' from Cromwell's armies, and Monmouth had brought over a Dutch gunner to take charge of the cannon. Monmouth had few weapons, apart from those that he had brought over from Holland. Former weapons of the Civil War were brought out of cupboards, others were manufactured by local blacksmiths. The pikemen in many cases used farm scythes, lashed to long poles. Training of the volunteers was a priority. Monmouth had arrived with 85 men, in five days his force had grown to over 3,000. Many of the volunteers came from the surrounding towns and villages. Colyton, a small Devon town provided 25% of its available male population, of which 75% were over the age of 25 years, which was comparatively old, perhaps demonstrating the degree of popularity and the area's commitment to Monmouth's cause. From Taunton 300 men joined. Once again the majority of the rebels were over twenty-five, when one would have thought they would have been married and settled down and unwilling to gamble home, family and in many cases their lives.

THE BATTLE OF BRIDPORT

On June 14th a small force was dispatched by Monmouth to deal with the local militia at Bridport. The force was to be under the command of Lord Grey. The troop consisted of 400 foot soldiers and 40 cavalry. They approached Bridport in the early hours of the morning taking the outlying Royalist militia sentries by surprise. The militia force consisted of 1200 foot soldiers and 100 horses, who were camped at the eastern end of the town. Monmouth's forces captured the western section of Bridport and the foot soldiers set off to attack the main militia force, with Lord Grey in support to the rear, with the cavalry. The main rebel group advanced on the militia who stood firm, after some initial nervousness. Volleys of musket shot were exchanged and the battle seemed in deadlock, until the rebels were fired on from the Bull Inn, which was halfway down the High Street. The rebels were now trapped at one end of the town. The cavalry, with Lord Grey had bolted, and headed back towards Lyme. Venner, one of the rebel leaders, though wounded, gave orders for the retreat. The retreat was orderly and Wade and Venner eventually led the rebel group back to Lyme and the main army.

Royalist Soldier

LORD ALBERMARLE AND THE
DUKE OF SOMERSET

Lord Albermarle and the Duke of Somerset were in charge of the nearest crown force; their instructions from London were to stop Monmouth's army leaving the town of Lyme. Albermarle came from Exeter to join forces with the Duke of Somerset. Monmouth was aware of this dangerous pincer movement that would cut him off from any outside help and prepared to leave. His army marched out of Lyme Regis at 10 a.m. on June 15th, heading towards Axminster.

THE MARCH FROM LYME REGIS TO TAUNTON

Lord Albermarle learnt of Monmouth's departure from Lyme and marched from Honiton to block the rebel advance. Monmouth reached Axminster, then a small market town on the Exeter and Taunton junction, first.

From Axminster Monmouth could clearly see the Royalist army advance from the west and his men prepared in battle formation. Lord Albermarle's force largely consisted of the local Devon militia, many of whom had considerable sympathy for the rebel cause. When only a quarter of a mile from Axminster Albermarle, fearing a mutiny from his untried militia, ordered a retreat. The Devon militia fell back in a panic with hardly a shot fired. Monmouth resumed the march into Taunton, so missing an early opportunity for a victory and a new supply of Royalist ammunition and weapons.

In London, James ordered road blocks to be set up to stop any more rebels joining Monmouth. Militias across the country were alerted and put in defensive positions. The Surrey militia was sent to Croydon to protect the southern flank of London, and a squadron was raised at Oxford to fight the Duke. Potential supporters were imprisoned or detained. A Royalist army, under Lord Churchill, marched with great speed and arrived in Bridport on the 17th June. Under his command he had two troops of dragoons and a regiment of cavalry. On June 18th, Monmouth marched into an undefended Taunton and was welcomed by the town. A force of local men had been raised to fight with the rebels and a group of young ladies had made a colour standard for them, which was received with great ceremony by Monmouth. There was one pressing problem that worried him, for while he had the support of the working and middle classes, few of the rich landowning nobility came forward to support the rebel cause. Therefore, it was decided to proclaim Monmouth King, in the hope of attracting more of the nobility to the cause. This was done at Taunton on June 20th 1685. In the proclamation, he accused James II of many crimes and offered a £500 reward to any who could bring James to Monmouth — dead or alive. This was a double insult, as at least James offered £5,000 for the head of Monmouth.

After the proclamation, Monmouth wrote to Lord Albermarle at Honiton, where he was awaiting the arrival of Churchill's regular soldiers. The letter was both cheeky and in a sad way amusing. Monmouth informed Albermarle, that as he was now the proclaimed 'King', he and his troops should come over and join his army, where they would be well treated. If he did not, then Monmouth would proclaim him a rebel and traitor. Albermarle replied, assuring Monmouth of his loyalty to James II, and advising Monmouth to give up the rebellion. His closing words were: "I do not doubt the justness of my cause shall sufficiently convince you that you had better have this rebellion alone, and not have put this nation to so much trouble!"

The proclamation of Monmouth as King failed to have the desired effect. Few of the nobility joined Monmouth, most still regarding him as illegitimate and therefore an imposter to the crown. The proclamation also upset many republicans who longed for the return of Cromwell's glorious commonwealth.

In the trail of Monmouth, were the regular troopers under Churchill, who had reached Chard, while Lord Albermarle had moved to Wellington with his militia force, which had regrouped after the Axminster debacle.

Monmouth's army marched out of Taunton on the 21st June and headed for Bridgwater. The Crown forces, with no intelligence clear as to Monmouth's intent, divided their forces to protect Bristol, Exeter and Bath. Monmouth's forces had now grown to over 7,000 strong, though many lacked any arms apart from staves, and these troops were yet to be tested in battle.

FROM TAUNTON TO BRISTOL —
JUNE 21st TO JUNE 24th

Monmouth had spent three days in the security of Taunton, but now the Royalist forces were snapping at his heels. There had been a number of skirmishes between protecting pickets and Royalist cavalry in the surrounding countryside. At one clash, a Yeovil man named Jarvis who was a rebel soldier was captured and hung by Churchill. Whilst in Taunton, Monmouth had restocked and reprovisioned his army; more men came forward to join though many were turned back due to the lack of weapons. Fortunately, a small catchment had been discovered in the Church tower of St. Mary's in Taunton, where the local militia had left many of their weapons when fleeing from Monmouth's approach.

Monmouth departed from Taunton on the 21st of June, marching north towards the Somerset town of Bridgwater, where the Duke of Monmouth was received by the town mayor, Alexander Popham and the local magistrates. The Duke stayed at Bridgwater castle while his troops camped in the surrounding fields. The next day the rebel army moved on to Glastonbury, passing through the town of Westonzoyland via Sedgemoor. At Glastonbury, the weather deteriorated and the rain fell. The rebels quartered in the Abbey buildings. Monmouth's plan was to attack and take Bristol — though time was fast running out. In Scotland, the Earl of Argyll's rebellion had failed. In the south Churchill's troops were hard on the heels of the rebel army, to the east the Duke of Grafton with the foot guards, were marching towards Monmouth. Monmouth was 26 miles away from Bristol, Grafton 60 miles. James II was desperate to delay Monmouth, so that his army could muster and attack the rebel forces. The only viable crossing point to Bristol over the river Avon was at Keynsham. He ordered the destruction of its bridge, which he hoped would delay Monmouth for two crucial days. Monmouth's delay was the turning point of the campaign.

On the 24th June the rebel army reached Pensford, just 12 miles from Bristol. Bristol had a history as a centre of dissidents and potential rebels. If Monmouth could have captured the city he would have been able to increase his army and have a strong base which contained the necessary weaponry and ordnance for the campaign against James.

From Pensford, Monmouth sent a Captain Tilley with a squadron of cavalry to Keynsham to inspect and repair the damaged bridge. As the rebel forces

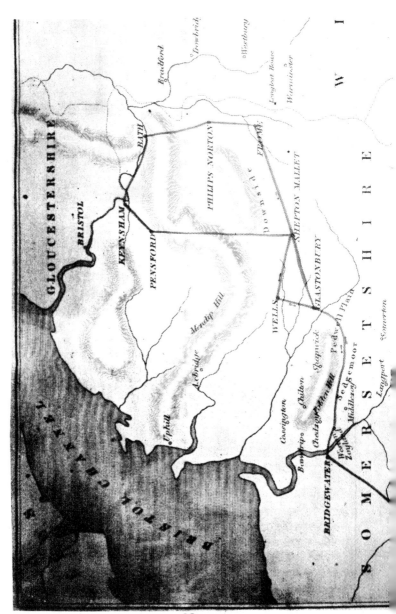

GLOUCESTERSHIRE

BRISTOL

KEYNSHAM

PENSFORD

BATH

PHILIPS NORTON

Bradford

Trowbridge

Westbury

Longleat House

Warminster

W I

Frome R.

Downside

SHEPTON MALLET

GLASTONBURY

WELLS

Mendip Hill

A.bridge

Uphill

Chilton

Edington

Chedzoy

Wedmore Hill

Pedwell Plain

Sedgemoor

Middlezoy

Weston Zoyland

Chedington

Bawdrip

BRIDGEWATER

Langport

Somerton

S O M E R S E T S H I R E

BRISTOL CHANNEL

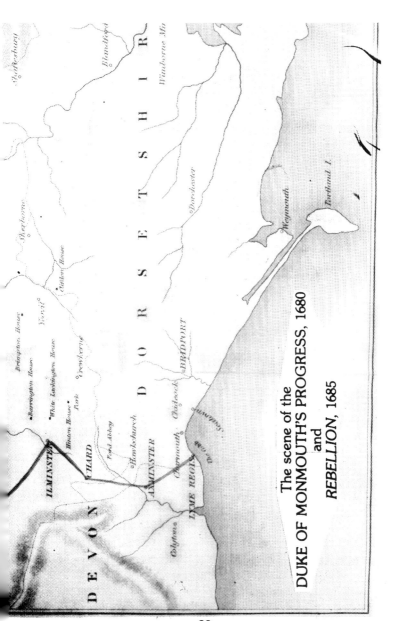

The scene of the
DUKE OF MONMOUTH'S PROGRESS, 1680
and
REBELLION, 1685

approached, a troop of militia forces fled in panic. By lunchtime, Tilley had repaired the bridge and the rebel army had crossed into Gloucester. Monmouth proposed to attack Bristol that night but there was no shelter on the western side of the Avon, so Monmouth marched his men back across the river to rest up and shelter from the rain, leaving only a few troops of scouting cavalry. During that evening at Keynsham, while the rebels laid plans to capture Bristol, two troops of Royalist cavalry raided the camp in an uncoordinated attack. From the east came a troop under the command of Colonel Oglethorp, while from Bristol another troop of cavalry led by Captain Parker had swum the Avon with their horses to attack the resting rebels. During the confusion of the lightning raid many rebels were killed or wounded. Some of the Royalist cavalry were captured by the rebels and questioned by Monmouth. The information obtained was of a large Royalist force not far from Keynsham which alarmed the Duke, who consequently wished to leave the area and forgo his plans to besiege Bristol. The fact was —the Royalist forces numbered just over 2,000, half the size of Monmouth's rebel army.

With no clear direction or intent Monmouth led his forces away in manoeuvres beginning to resemble a ramble round the West Country, whilst the Royalist forces, no longer fragmented were unifying into a coordinated and strong force. Churchill had arrived with his regular troops from London, via Dorset, after tailing Monmouth from Lyme Regis and Lord Grafton (Monmouth's half brother) had arrived from London with the seasoned and experienced Dumbarton regiment and their cannons. Lord Faversham at last had an army of regular troops and no longer needed to rely on the inexperienced local militias.

AFTER KEYNSHAM......

From the catastrophe of Keynsham the rebels marched on to Bath where the gates to the city were slammed at their approach. The march from Keynsham had been long and tiring and time was too short to lay siege to the well fortified town. Monmouth led his army away from Bath deciding to head for the Somerset town of Frome. Throughout the march the rebels were continuously harassed by the Royalist cavalry. Rumours were rife among the rebel army and no doubt many were by now homesick. The indecisiveness of Monmouth did little to raise the spirits or morale of his men and some of them started to desert.

Monmouth rested midway for the night at the small village of Norton St. Philip, commandeering the local inn, The George, as his headquarters. It was while resting at the inn that an attempt was made to assassinate the Duke. As he stood at the window a musket was fired, but the shot went wide of him. The bullet was alleged to have been a silver button. The would-be assassin was able to vanish in the confusion, technically unable to claim the £5,000 reward for the death of the Duke which was an expensive shot to miss!

THE BATTLE OF NORTON ST. PHILIP

Lord Faversham soon learnt that the rebel army was resting at the small village of Norton St. Philip. He sent a force under the command of Lord Grafton to engage the rebels. Monmouth's sentries soon saw the approaching Royalist column of 500 soldiers. A defence was hastily planned and the rebels deployed behind the hedgerows with their muskets to await the advance of the King's army up the main road into the village, which was now barricaded. Lord Grafton marched into the trap, and was soon cut off as musket fire peppered his troops. It was only the valiant cavalry charge, led by Churchill that opened up a route for

THE GEORGE INN NORTON ST PHILIP

26

retreat. In the battle Lord Grafton had lost over 100 men while the rebels lost 18. The rebels pressed home their advantage chasing and firing at the retreating soldiers, though gradually they lost the protection of the hedgerows as they came to more open country.

The rebels were careful to avoid a skirmish with the Royalist cavalry and a stalemate ensued. Rebel and Royalist duelled with each other, from distances too far apart to do much harm. The battle of Norton St. Philip had been a success for the rebels, but once again Monmouth had failed to take advantage of the situation.

With neither side wishing to fight a conclusive battle the Royalist forces retired to Bradford-on-Avon while the rebels, fearing a counter-attack, moved on from Norton through the night to Frome. They left a small picket at Norton to construct camp fires and so deceive the Royal scouts as to the true location of their forces.

FROME 28th JUNE

It must have been a very wet, tired and quiet army that marched into Frome, though it was well received by the town. Monmouth was now short on ammunition and needed more weapons for his army, neither of which was available in Frome. It was in this small Somerset market town that Monmouth learnt of the defeat Argyll and his Scottish rebellion and news also came that further reinforcements of cannon and men were leaving London destined for Faversham's army. Despite the recent success of Norton St. Philip, Monmouth's morale sagged and he even discussed abandoning his cause, fleeing to Poole and crossing back to the Continent. His advisers were divided, though Lord Grey's countenance prevailed and it was decided to fight on. The planned march on London was no longer possible; with fresh reinforcements coming from London the Royalist army had effectively

27

blocked the rebels to the southwest. News of an uprising at Axbridge and mustering of new recruits at Bridgwater determined the plan of action. Monmouth was to lead his army back to Bridgwater.

FROM FROME TO SHEPTON MALLET, WELLS AND BRIDGWATER

From Frome the rebels marched to Shepton Mallet. The Royalist army soon moved into the town in their wake. From the market square a proclamation was read which offered a pardon to any rebels who would lay down their weapons and return home. Monmouth and his officers tried desperately to keep news of the pardon from the men, fearing desertions on a large scale. A blacksmith was hung by Monmouth for having a copy of the pardon in his possession at Bridgwater.

It was another short march to the Cathedral town of Wells, arriving on July 1st. As no ammunition or weapons were found in the town the roof of the Cathedral was stripped of its lead to be made into shot for the muskets. A militant section of the rebels, remembering Cromwell's persecution of the church set about mutilating the carvings and statues at the front of the building, which many associated with the spread of Popery. It was only the intervention of Lord Grey and a group of officers that spared the Cathedral from greater damage. They chased the rebel vandals from the church.

JULY 2nd

After resting at Wells Monmouth left on the morning of July 2nd, still hoping to obtain more weapons and enlist the rumoured band of recruits mustering in Bridgwater. Nearby at Minehead were some cannon which he now needed to collect, to supplement his own meagre force. However, their cool reception in Bridgwater was disappointing and the number of new recruits hardly made up for those who had deserted. The rebels were weary, always aware of the stalking royal army, their rearguard harassed by cavalry, and their morale was low.

BRIDGWATER 3rd JULY

A few miles to the east of Bridgwater regiments of
the Royalist army were camped on the open moor and
in the small hamlets. Back in Bridgwater Monmouth
set about preparing for a siege. He constructed

Severall Officers by Command
of y' King going into y' West

the Late D: of M: writing
a letter to y' D of Albermarl

The D of Grafton &c fighting their
way through sever of y Rebels horse
in y lane leading to Philips Norton

The Battaile att Bridgwater

earthen ramparts, barricaded roads and strengthened the defences of the town. Lord Faversham was unsure of Monmouth's strategy and suspected it could be a front, to cover a withdrawal, allowing them to move further to the west, or make a sudden strike to the north at Bristol. Faversham's own men were tired after the wearisome game of 'cat and mouse' across Somerset. His regular soldiers had scarcely recovered from the sudden march from London. The battle experiences of Norton St. Philip had undermined his confidence and a more cautious approach was needed. Thus it was decided to rest the Royal army, but to block any possible advance to Bristol by positioning the cannon on the main roads to the north.

Monmouth learnt of the deployment and proximity of the resting Royal army from the local graziers who knew the area. From the church tower of St. Mary's it was possible to see their tents through his spy glass. Monmouth planned some decisive strategy to press forward his advantage.

Lord Faversham had set up his headquarters in the hamlet of Westonzoyland, he had camped with the cavalry of the Lifeguards and the Blues. At Middlezoy, a mile to the south east Lord Pembroke was camped with the men of the Wiltshire militia and between the two hamlets of Westonzoyland and Chedzoy, out on to the open moor, were the 2,000 regular soldiers. The Royalist army was only 5 miles from the rebels.

The whole town knew of Monmouth's preparations; it was a miracle that Lord Faversham did not! On 5th July Monmouth gave the order for attack.

THE PREPARATION AND MARCH TO SEDGEMOOR

The preparation for the coming battle began in earnest. Muskets were loaded and sword and scythes were sharpened but there was not time to fetch the sea defence cannon from Minehead. Monmouth, in consultation with his commanders planned the attack. The Duke through his local intelligence of graziers and farmers knew the disposition of the sleeping Royal army. Monmouth was to march with his men later that night towards the Royalist camp whilst the men were sleeping. The cavalry, under the command of Lord Grey would cross over the two wide drainage channels, which separated the opposing armies. Their guides were to be local graziers who knew the location of the causeways. Once across, the cavalry would tear into the sleeping camp and attempt to take the cannon. In the confusion of the onslaught, Monmouth and his remaining footsoldiers would line the opposing bank of the nearest channel, rack the camp with musket fire and sweep in for the final attack. The plan was simple and bold though it would need the element of complete surprise to achieve its ultimate goal. With the Royalist army defeated London and Bristol would be open, and no doubt further rebellion would have been sparked off elsewhere in the kingdom.

The orders were given and the rebel farmers and yeomen assembled later that evening and marched out of Bridgwater. The night was misty and dark, Lord Faversham in the small village of Westonzoyland was unprepared and his outlying scouts and pickets inadequate. His force of cannon were set to guard the deserted road to Bristol. Even the sentries failed to hear the quiet approach of over 3,000 rebels.

THE BATTLE OF SEDGEMOOR

The rebels marched out of Bridgwater at eleven o'clock on Sunday, July 5th, 1685. The moon though full was shielded by a mantle of mist and fog. The rebels marched in complete silence; the column of men, horses and wagons stretching back over a mile. They took the Bristol road out of Bridgwater, turned off two miles from the town, and took to the unguarded, smaller lanes. With the noise of wagons

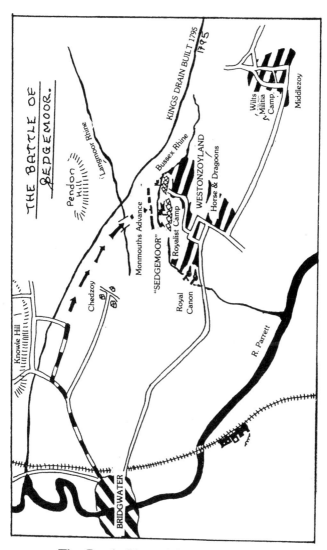

The Battle Plan of Sedgemoor 1685

33

and horses it is a wonder that Faversham was not forewarned. In the Royalist camp most men were asleep. Only the Dumbarton regiment had stacked their muskets outside their tents for immediate use. The rebel cavalry, under Lord Grey, went ahead of the footsoldiers. They crossed the first drainage ditch (Langmoor Rhine), though the crossing had taken much longer than expected, then the local guide failed to find the causeway. With some of the rebel force across, the cavalry sped on towards the second crossing. Suddenly a shot rang out, from one of the patrolling Royalist cavalry pickets who then rode back to the sleeping camp to warn of Monmouth's approach. Having raised the alarm, drums were wildly beating while men stumbled about in panic groping for their weapons. Lord Grey and his cavalry made a dash for the second causeway across the last remaining drainage ditch, but they ran into a body of Royalist cavalry. Lord Grey charged, wounding the Royalist commander. The returning volley of fire scattered the rebel cavalry and the majority fled the field of battle in disray. A smaller group of rebel cavalry reformed under the command of Captain Jones and attacked in an attempt to try and capture the crossing into the Royal Camp. But again they were repulsed. The failure of the cavalry to cross the Bussex Rhine threw the rebels' planned strategy into total confusion. The main body of rebels, still a considerable distance from the opening battle speeded up their march. The leading regiment of men under the command of Colonel Wade was the first to reach the Bussex Rhine. They had become detached from the following regiments. Wade and his men arrived at the edge of the Bussex Rhine, and were preparing to charge, when the second regiment came up and proceeded to lay down on the banks and fire across the water into the Royalist camp. The rebel advance had collapsed, and there was no chance of Wade's men charging the camp with the other rebels firing from the rear. It was dark and in the confusion communication between regiments was impossible. There was general panic and flight and even the waggon drivers, with their vital supplies of ammunition and powder abandoned their posts. Those rebels moving forward created more congestion and confusion as the musket battle raged along the banks of the Bussex Rhine. The untrained and undisciplined rebels fired indiscriminately into the darkened Royalist camp, using up powder and shot. However, the rebel cannon under the command of a Dutch mercenary did great damage and caused many casualties. The Royalist cannon at the time was misaligned and out of range of the rebels.

As dawn approached the position was stalemate and Monmouth's army was unable to advance or retreat, as they no longer had cavalry protection to guard their flanks. The tide of the battle was turning; the rebels had lost momentum. Lord Faversham then brought into action his cannons which were more numerous than those of the rebels. Soon the rebel cannon was silenced and numbers of men fell as grape shot tore into their ranks. It was later in the morning that Colonel Oglethorp and his cavalry were able to make their way round to the rear of the rebel army. Shortly before the final onslaught Monmouth had decided that the cause was lost; he and Lord Grey hastily abandoned their body armour and fled from the battle, while many of their rebels bravely fought on. The first charge by Colonel Oglethorp and his cavalry was repulsed, the rebel pikemen holding their ground. The second charge destroyed the rebel force which broke up in disarray. The Royalists' charged across the Bussex Rhine and the carnage continued. Only Wade and his men were able to leave the field in an orderly retreat. Many were cut down by the cavalry and hacked to pieces when caught hiding in the cornfields. Over 500 prisoners were locked up in the church at Westonzoyland. Lord Faversham celebrated his victory by hanging twenty-two prisoners from a nearby tree. The army was encouraged to inflict retribution on the captured rebels. A few days after the battle Lord Faversham was summoned to London to receive the King's congratulations. In his place was appointed Colonel Kirk of the Tangier Regiment, a man with a fearsome reputation for savagery. In Taunton he hanged twenty prisoners. He allowed his men to plunder and take the spoils of war and he sold pardons to the richer rebels. He was later rebuked by James who preferred to see them hung. After the battle those rebels lucky enough to escape broke up into smaller groups and attempted to make their way home. Rewards were offered for the capture of any rebels. Many chose to live in the woods and moors of Dorset, Somerset and Devon. Some groups such as Wade's were large enough to fight-off any pursuers, though Wade was later captured in Lynmouth after a failed attempt to take command of a ship.

Wade was eventually pardoned by James for his part in the rebellion, though many were less fortunate. The prisons and jails of the West Country were full with rebels.

THE FLIGHT OF MONMOUTH

The Duke of Monmouth, Lord Grey and a man called Buyse fled the battle when all seemed lost. The group had decided to make their way through Somerset and into Dorset and eventually to Poole hoping to obtain passage back to the Continent.

QUEEN ♣

The Defeat of the Rebells 2000 Slayn & their Canon taken

V ♦

Severall of ỹ Rebells hang'd upon a Tree

VII ♦

the Lᵈ Gray taken in Difguise

KING ♣

Goodenough Coll Holmes &c under Examination

Meanwhile a reward of £8,000 was offered for the capture of Monmouth.

Such a large inducement caused the local militias to search with considerable enthusiasm. The group travelled across Somerset by night avoiding the larger towns and villages. Near Gillingham they obtained the services of a guide called Richard Hollyday, who was to try and lead them to the coast of Dorset. They travelled southwards through Cranbourne Chase (modern spelling) stopping at Woodyates Inn. Twenty-four hours after the battle they rested and changed. Monmouth dressed as a shepherd, a disguise he hoped would blend into the countryside. But, unwisely he could not bear to leave his Royal Garter, snuff box and gold guineas behind. He put them into the pockets of his trousers. Leaving the horses at the inn they set on the long walk to the coast.

7th JULY 1685

Two days after the battle the fugitives left the inn. They were now travelling in daylight hours. At Wimborne St. Giles, later that day, the group decided to separate. Lord Grey and Robert Hollyday were captured soon after, at the village of Holt, by men from the Sussex militia. Buyse and Monmouth were seen in a copse of thick vegetation, at Horton Heath, near Ringwood, by a peasant woman who told some passing members of the militia. Buyse was caught first and it is thought that Buyse probably told his capturers of the whereabouts of the Duke, as he was eventually pardoned. The men from the Sussex militia found Monmouth hiding in a ditch (2 miles from the village of Horton in Hampshire). It was the early morning of the 8th of July. At first Monmouth denied he was a rebel, but when searched they found the money and Royal Garter he had carefully kept, and not far away was the snuff box.

MONMOUTH'S FATE

Monmouth, Grey and Buyse were taken to London. Monmouth was desperate to elude his fate. He had already been condemned to death by Parliament for treason. He wrote to anyone who had influence with James, even the Queen Mother, but all to no avail. He asked for an audience with the King. James granted his request, though it was the custom that the condemned only saw the face of the monarch to receive a pardon. Monmouth was reputed to have thrown himself at the feet of James and begged for clemency, but James remained adamant that Monmouth was to be executed. After this meeting Monmouth was resigned to his fate and set about preserving the social position of his family from the revenge of the King. In return for a public letter denying right to the throne James allowed Monmouth's wife to keep her estates.

On the 15th of July 1685 Monmouth was led out of the Tower of London onto the scaffolding; the crowd was large and many were sympathetic towards him. Before Monmouth placed his head on the block, he gave the axeman, John Ketch six guineas and told him to perform his work well. The first blow barely made a gash in the Duke's neck, the second blow cut only a little deeper. The crowd grew restive and it was on the fourth blow that Monmouth's head was severed from his neck. Monmouth's body was spared the indignity of quartering and was laid to rest in the cemetery of the Tower.

THE BLOODY ASSIZES

In the Autumn of 1685 the King sent Judge Jeffreys to punish the rebels through the power of the courts and to make examples of those found guilty.

The prisons and jails of Somerset, Devon and Dorset were full. After the rebellion the local parish constables were instructed to report those who had been absent during the period of Monmouth's march, rebellion and defeat, but though many rebels and sympathisers were arrested many escaped as some parish constables made incomplete returns or names were removed from the list by bribery.

Lord Chief Justice, George, Baron, Jeffreys.
Judge Jeffreys was born in Acton near Wrexham, in Wales. The son of a local gentleman. Jeffreys was sent to Westminster Public School, and on leaving he went into law and eventually became Recorder for London. He was appointed Lord Chief Justice by Charles II. Judge Jeffreys was renowned for his bad temper, which many thought was due to the kidney stones that plagued his health. In court he had a bullying manner that cowered the defence. He was a man of sharp tongue and little patience.

THE TRIAL OF DAME ALICE LISLE,
25th AUGUST 1685, WINCHESTER

The first court of the Autumn Assizes was at Winchester and among the cases was that of Dame Alice Lisle. She was charged with aiding and abetting the escape of two rebels, the first being John Hicks, a dissenting minister and the second a lawyer called Melthorp. Though strangely, at the time of the trial neither of the two men had been found guilty of taking part in the rebellion. Anyway Dame Alice was over eighty, deaf and with bad eyesight. As a show trial it was a disaster, for the jury failed three times to come to a verdict. The case for the defence was that at the time Dame Alice did not know that the two men had been involved in the rebellion at Sedgemoor. Jeffreys pressurised the jury to record a verdict of 'guilty of treason'. He sentenced Dame Alice to die by burning at the stake, although after an appeal to James this was later commuted to beheading. She was eventually executed in the market place at Winchester.

SALISBURY ASSIZES

There were few rebels to try at Salisbury though six people were sentenced to be fined and whipped for 'uttering seditious words'.

DORCHESTER ASSIZES, 3rd SEPTEMBER 1685

At Dorchester there were over three hundred people indicted to appear. The trials started on the 5th of September. The first thirty to be tried all entered pleas of 'not guilty', however, all but one was found 'guilty'. It was up to those pleading 'not guilty' to prove that they took no part in the rebellion, so in effect they were guilty until proved innocent. The crown produced witnesses of dubious character to gain convictions. All the twenty-nine found guilty were sentenced to death and to be hanged the next day, but the hangman was only able to execute 13, as the work load was too great.

Jeffreys made it clear that those pleading innocence would be executed if found guilty. The next day Jeffreys heard a hundred and three cases all of whom pleaded guilty. A sentence of death was passed on them all and eighty were hanged in various parts of Dorset, for the rest the death sentence was remitted to a whipping or transportation to the colonies, as slaves. Among the more famous prisoners tried were Richard Hollyday, Monmouth's guide as he fled from the battle. On the 8th of September a further sixty-nine cases were heard, once again there were few acquittals, though a number of richer rebels were able to buy their freedom by bribing Jeffreys. The assize ended on the 10th September. The sentencing at Dorchester was the harshest of the assizes. Over 90 were executed, 175 were sentenced to transportation, 55 were pardoned while only 15 were set free. The executions were spread across the Dorset towns and at Lyme Regis twelve were hanged on the spot that Monmouth had landed. After hanging the victim was cut down barely dead, disembowelled and quartered. The quarters were tarred to preserve them for public display. From Dorchester Jeffreys passed through Lyme where he was entertained at a Council banquet. The next day he moved on to Devon and the assizes at Exeter.

EXETER ASSIZES, 14th SEPTEMBER

There were four hundred and eighty people indicted to appear at the assizes though only forty appeared to be tried. A further three hundred and forty-two could not be traced, and many were probably still hiding in the woods and moors of Devon. Of the forty on trial only twenty eight were tried as rebels, the others were being tried for supporting Monmouth. Twelve were executed at the main Devon market towns while the others were either sentenced to transportation or whipping.

TAUNTON ASSIZES, 18th SEPTEMBER

The assizes opened at Taunton Castle. Somerset was the heart of the rebellion. There were over one thousand indicted to appear though only five hundred

VIII

Bonfires made the 26 of July at night being the thanksgiving for the Victory. 1685

VII

The late D of M beheaded on Tower Hill 15 July 1685

II

Severall Rebells tryed in the West.

III

Major Holmes and 2 other Rebells Hanged in Chaines

Many of those sentenced to death had this commuted to transportation. The sale of the convicts to plantation owners brought a considerable amount of exchange to the crown. The wealth and property of the rebels were confiscated. In Somerset over two hundred were sentenced to hang, with the emphasis on the executions taking place at the towns which had given Monmouth support. The total number of rebels executed in Somerset was about one hundred and fifty, as many escaped the hangman's noose, by masquerading as other prisoners or by breaking out of prison.

From Taunton the assizes moved to Wells, where there were more rebels to be tried.

THE WELLS ASSIZES, 23rd SEPTEMBER

At Wells there were nearly 500 prisoners for trial. Most were intimidated into pleading guilty and subsequently sentenced to death, ninety-seven were hanged and nearly 400 transported for sale on the colonies. After a further assize at Bristol, where there were only a few rebels Jeffreys returned to London. He came back considerably richer from the bribes he had taken, having abided by the King's wishes and inflicted terror into the hearts of any potential rebels. The market towns of Dorset, Somerset and Devon displayed the tarred quarters of executed rebels and folk from these rebellious counties were cowered into submission. Judge Jeffreys was rewarded by the King and appointed as Lord High Chancellor of England.